WARYAM SINGH 'KHALIFA'

Narinda Singh Dhesi

The Naval & Military Press Ltd

Published by

The Naval & Military Press Ltd
Unit 5 Riverside, Brambleside
Bellbrook Industrial Estate
Uckfield, East Sussex
TN22 1QQ England

Tel: +44 (0) 1825 749494

www.naval-military-press.com

© Copyright Narinda Singh Dhesi

WARYAM SINGH 'KHALIFA'

Narindar Singh Dhesi

Khalifa

"We came in Dhows"

Khalifa

Waryam Singh 'Khalifa'
(1888-1978)

Gurbachan Kaur
(1908- 2008)

Khalifa

My father Waryam Singh was born in 1888, in the village of Sang Dhesian in the Punjab to Bhola Singh and Chand Kaur, a Jatt (cultivators) family of Sikhs. I could not trace any family linage beyond Bhola Singh. My father was the youngest of seven children: two girls and five boys. My grandfather passed away when my father was nine years old.

He was very close to one sister called Atri Kaur, who married a farmer of Mathida Clan. One of our father's brothers became a Sant (holy man) and became a wanderer. He did not leave any trace. One brother, the father of Buta Singh, passed away. Two brothers died in the Plague of 1892 at Lyallpur, now in Pakistan. (The city was renamed "Faisalabad" in honour of King Faisal of Saudi Arabia.) The newly-created Lyallpur district was carved out of Gujranwala, Jhang and Lahore districts. It was a newly created canal colony which was settled by Jatt farmers. On the death of his brothers the land was offered to our father, but our grandmother refused to part with her only surviving son and the land lapsed back to the Punjab government.

On his father's and brothers' deaths his ancestral farming land at Sang Dhesian was wrested from him by the village Zaildar (Zaildar was a native officer in charge of a village in the colonial rural administration of Punjab in British India).

He was raised by our grandmother in utter poverty. Most of the time, he was physically abused and made to work for food. As a child he was befriended by one Karam Singh Dhesi, nicknamed Madhoo, who became his mentor. Time went by and our father grew up to be a tall strong young man and he decided to re-claim his ancestral land. He approached the Zaildar and was turned away with a torrent of abuse. So he decided to take matters in his own hands. He borrowed a set of bullocks from one of the villagers and started ploughing his land. He also attached a wooden Dang (a staff) to the plough, to fend off any person or persons who might want to stop him in his work. While ploughing his land, the village Zaildar approached him and subjected him to the choicest of Punjabi abuse and physically tried to eject him from his land.

Khalifa

In the altercation, my father hit the Zaildar with the staff and the Zaildar dropped dead. To fend off the influential Zaildar family and the authorities, and with hardly any family ties, my father hurriedly left the village in 1904. He made his way to the coastal city of Bombay (renamed Mumbai, the capital city of the Indian state of Maharashtra). At that time people from the Punjab were heading for Bombay, hoping to catch a ship and migrate to other parts of the British Empire and the Americas. The main port and the labour recruiters for the colonies were based at Bombay. He was sixteen years old. Being a tall Sikh young man he managed to get a job as a security guard at a Bank on Marine Drive in Bombay. At the same time East African Railways were recruiting artisans and labourers to work on the construction of the Uganda Railways in Kenya. Some five or six Ramgharia Sikhs, (Artisans) named Kalsi, from his village had been recruited as artisans by the Uganda Railways and had made their way to Bombay for embarkation to Kenya. As he was on guard duty one day, he recognized the Kalsis, who were out for a walk on Marine Drive.

He approached them and they suggested to him that the best way for him was to pretend to be a Kalsi and join them on the trip to Kenya, which he did. In 1905 my father, with the Kalsis, travelled from Bombay to Mombasa in what I believe was a dhow, which took about forty five days. He was seventeen years old.

On their journey there were some Ramgharia Sikhs, a few Jatt Sikhs and the rest of the group was made up of Harijans (Lower Caste). The Ramgarhias and Jatts had segregated themselves from the Harijans with separate kitchens. It was quite a long journey during which the Ramgharia and Jatt food ran out. They had to join the Harijans in sharing their food and the caste barriers of the group were shattered.

From Mombasa my father ended up in Nairobi where he was employed by the 'Uganda Railways'. The line was 582 miles long. It began on the Mombasa mainland and it reached Port Florence on Lake Victoria.

Khalifa

India agreed to provide labour only on condition that every emigrant, at the end of three years service, would be afforded the threefold option of renewing his contract, returning to his home village with all expenses paid, or remaining in East Africa as a settler and forfeiting his return passage. A total of 34,400 Asians worked on the construction of the Mombasa–Kisumu segment. The official historian of the Railway went even further in his forthright comment: "Without the aid of Indian labour, artisans and subordinate staff, the railway would not have been built"!

Our father was employed as a rivet banger on the railway cars in the railway workshops at Nairobi. After some time he graduated to be a Boilermaker in the local workshop. As farming was still in his blood, while at Nairobi, he acquired a small farm on the outskirts of the town on River Road and also set up a gym to teach fellow Sikhs wrestling, as he had become an expert wrestler. Apart from Kenyan wrestlers, many wrestlers visiting Kenya came to wrestle there. However, none of them could defeat our father in wrestling, so the people gave him the title of *Khalifa*. (The name Khalifa is of Arabic origin and means "one who succeeds")

At this time there was Tug of War competition arranged between the Sikhs and Punjabi Muslims. Considering the centuries old antagonism between the two communities, it was a fierce strength of arms. The Sikhs, with our father competing, just managed to win by a whisker. During the Tug of War, there were handful of Hindus, whose sympathies traditionally should have been with the Sikhs, but as a mischief, were cheering the Muslims. At the end of the Tug of War, our father dragged these Hindus to the local Gurdwara (Temple) and had them baptized to the Sikh faith!

Years passed in continuous employment. Most of the Sikh workers went back to the Punjab at the end of three years service. Our father was very apprehensive of returning back to the Punjab, as he thought that he would be apprehended by the authorities, for causing the death of the village Zaildar. However, he was reassured by some Sikh returnees, that as there had been no charges brought against him and the lapse of so many years since the altercation, no charges could be framed against him.

Khalifa

Eventually our father travelled back to India in 1925. He made his way to Sang Dhesian, where he built a house for himself in the village behind Kehar Singh Kalsi's house. New religious ideologies in the 20TH century had caused tensions in the Sikh religion. The Akali Dal (Army of the Immortals), a political-religious movement founded in 1920, preached a return to the roots of the Sikh religion. The Akali Dal became the political party which would articulate Sikh claims and lead the independence movement. One of the major campaigns in the Sikhs' agitation was for the reformation of their holy places. The campaign, which elicited enthusiastic support especially from the rural masses, took the form of a peaceful agitation-marches, religious gatherings (Jathas) and demonstrations for Sikhs to assert their right to manage their places of worship. This led to a series of mass arrests and imprisonments by the authorities. As the jails were overflowing with the religious internees, the people who fed these Jathas on their marches were also arrested and imprisoned. As one of the hungry Jathas was passing through his village, my father entertained them to a Langar, that is, he fed the hungry marchers. Our grandmother was certain that he would be arrested by the authorities for feeding the Jatha, and advised him that if he was given the option to apologies, he was not to, and face the consequences. The courage of our grandmother, who had not seen her surviving son for so many years, was amazing. Our father was arrested by the authorities. He was given the option to apologies, which he declined, and was sentenced and imprisoned for six months in Rawalpindi Jail (Now in Pakistan).

Rawalpindi Central Jail, 1920s.

Khalifa

In Rawalpindi Jail, my father was given a bag of grain to grind for the group. My father refused to grind the whole bag which was given to him, but for a couple of handfuls of grain, which he thought was sufficient for his needs.

Consequently he had a confrontation with the Jailer (a Muslim lifer who had been made a trustee). The trustee had been very abusive to the Sikhs. He threatened to tear off our father's beard and shove it in our father's backside. During the altercation, my father picked him up and threw him down. He cracked his head and died. My father was locked up in solitary confinement and the authorities were arranging to hang him. Most of the Sikh protesters, in various prisons (there were thousands of them) hearing of his imminent hanging, went on hunger strike. To stave off a mass rebellion and finding that my father had migrated to Kenya, the authorities allowed him to sort out his affairs, which included the marriage to our mother Gurbachan Kaur of Magsudpur village, Hoshiarpur District, Punjab (now in Pakistan). Then the authorities deported him to Kenya. In 1926 he journeyed back to Kenya with our mother and grandmother. He resumed his employment with the Kenya Railways for some time. Eventually he resigned from the Railways and moved to Makindu, where he became a fuel supplying contractor to the Railways. Makindu at that time was a dreary isolated village. The only place of note was the Railway Shed. Our parents lived in a mud hut on the outskirts of the village. While at Makindu my mother gave birth to a daughter, who unfortunately died at childbirth. Our mother tells us that a pride of lions use to come roaming around the huts at night time.

Khalifa

Mr Chuni Lal and his brother ran small general stores at Makindu, while Babu Tara Singh Ahluwalia was the station master. The Lal brothers, Babu Tara Singh and our father got together and collected some money from Nairobi Singh Sabha Gurdwara and built the Makindu Gurdwara, practically a tin roofed hut. Our father also planted some fruit cuttings which he had brought from the Punjab at the Gurdwara and I believe that the fruit trees are thriving to this day. On April 27, 1930, the new Gurdwara was opened at Makindu in the presence of about 150 Sikhs from East Africa. The new Gurdwara is described as "a magnificent stone building with fine arches at the front and back and a beautiful garden."

Today, all types of people visit this Gurdwara everyday and it is a "must-see" Gurdwara for any Sikh travelling to Kenya and East Africa. It provides a peaceful atmosphere where one can meditate and calm one's mind before proceeding to join the "rat-race" again. So the Sikh community of Kenya has done something special by building such a beautiful edifice and campus where anyone of any religion or of no religion can withdraw from the mundane and reflect on the spiritual. This large complex houses a huge dining facility which provides free Langar 24 hours a day, as determined by their founder Guru, Guru Nanak Dev.

Khalifa

In 1930 our father had a whole stack of wood ready to be picked up by the Railways that caught fire and got burnt. He could not sustain the losses and had to fold up his business. At the birth of my elder brother, Jaswant in 1931 at Makindu, our father moved to Kakamega with his nephew Buta Singh. On the eve of his deportation from India, he had adopted Buta Singh as his own son and had brought him with him to Kenya. On the move to Kakamega, my father and Buta Singh were employed by the Rosterman Goldmines as mechanical technicians. In due course Gurbaksh was born in Kakamega in 1934. In 1937 our father moved to Eldoret, where he worked for East African Power and Lighting Company. As the instinct and passion for farming had never left him, he also acquired a small farm in Eldoret. My elder brother Kulwant, I (Narindar) and my younger brother Surinder were born in Eldoret. As my older brother Jass was afflicted with Muscular Dystrophy my father thought that the climate in Mombasa might help and he got transferred to Mombasa in 1942, which of course did not help. In 1945, with the shortage of technicians in Uganda, he was transferred to Jinja to work for Uganda Electricity Board. My elder brother Jass passed away in 1949 in Jinja. The rest of us had an ideal upbringing and schooling in Jinja. In 1952 our father took the whole family to the Punjab for the arranged marriage of my elder brother Gurbaksh Singh to Randhir Kaur, daughter of Mehr Singh, who was a Zaildar of a prominent family of Jandiala village. As Lakha Singh (father's nephew) had sold the house that my father had built, we stayed in a mud house that my father had salvaged in the adjoining plot.

As his passion was for farming, he also acquired a small farm by Lake Victoria at Jinja adjacent to the old power station. There was an abundance of fresh vegetables and milk in our house! When the power station at the hydraulic dam became operational to supply electricity to the rest of Uganda, our father was transferred to the Owen falls hydraulic dam. Incidentally my elder brother Gurbaksh Singh worked on the Owen falls hydraulic dam, during its construction.

Khalifa

In 1956 while our father was working for Uganda Electricity Board at Owen Falls hydraulic dam, the Queen Mother performed the opening ceremony of the dam and the Power Station. During the ceremony our father Waryam Singh 'Khalifa' and one of his Sikh colleagues, Harjodh Singh were presented to the Queen Mother.

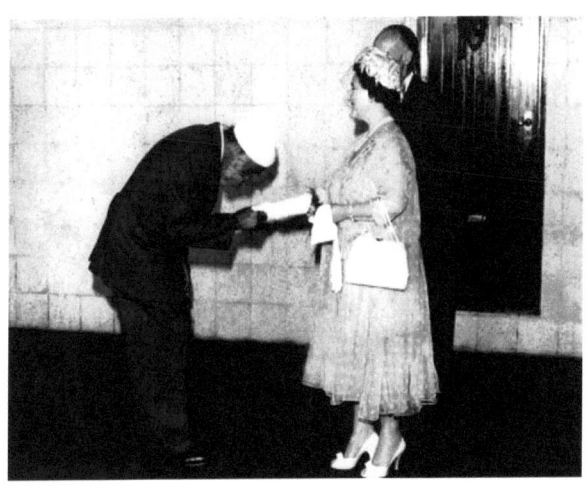

They were the only two Asians presented to her. In 1957 I absconded to England. Our father retired in 1963 and went back to his village in the Punjab, where he built a large house for his retirement.

Owen Falls power station and dam, Jinja.

Khalifa

My younger brother stayed in Uganda. Our brother Kulwant passed away at Sang Dhesian in the same year. Meanwhile I had joined the British Army and was serving in Bahrain, where my brother Gurbaksh traced me and told me about Kulwant's passing away. From Bahrain in late 1963, I travelled to Sang Dhesian via Pakistan to submerge my brother's ashes in the holy river. Our father felt nostalgic for Africa and came back to Uganda in 1966 and stayed with Gurbaksh for a year. On 4TH August 1972, the then President of Uganda, Idi Amin, ordered the expulsion of his country's Indian minority, giving them 90 days to leave Uganda. Gurbaksh left Uganda as a refugee and settled in Canada. My younger brother Surindar had migrated to England. After a few years Gurbaksh sponsored Surindar, who joined him in Canada. Our father had an ideal retirement and died peacefully at Sang Dhesian in 1978. Gurbaksh and I went to Sang Dhesian to do the funeral rites and brought our mother back with us. She went to Calgary in Canada with Gurbaksh and eventually stayed with Surindar, while Gurbaksh had migrated again, this time to the United States. Our mother passed away in Calgary in 2008. She is survived by her children and grandchildren and great grandchildren in England, Canada and United States.

The Family House is now:

Mamaji Gurbachan Kaur
Women Development Centre.

Khalifa

The house in Sang Dhesian was looked after for many years by a caretaker. After the death of our mother, her grandchildren wanted to leave a legacy for their grandmother. The house, in partnership with Baba Sang Dhesian Girls College in Dhesian, has been turned into a women's development centre, to provide education and life skills to girls and women of Sang Dhesian and surrounding areas who cannot afford to go to College. It bears the legacy of our mother who helped and nurtured many young women from the family during her stay in India.

Gurdwara Baba Sangji, Sang Dhesian

Khalsa College for Girls, Sang Dhesian

Khalifa

Family Genealogy

Bhola Singh-Chand Kaur
↓
Waryam Singh-Gurbachan Kaur
↓
Jaswant, Gurbaksh, Kalwant, Narindar, Surinder

Gurbaksh Singh-Randhir Kaur
▼
Rabindar (Gurinder), Meena (Sathi), Harveen (Grewal)
▼   ▼
Kevi (Mandeep), Neil (Soni)   Sahej
▼   ▼
Nikheel-Syra   Caspin

Narindar Singh-Beverley Turner
▼
Surindar (Rehman), Jodh (Ria), Jassa, Sher
▼
Laurie

Surinder Singh-Satwant Kaur
▼
Neetu (Harminder), Sandeep, Mandeep
↓
Sahil, Gurbir, Simran

Thana Singh - Man Kaur
▼
Kartar Kaur, *Gurbachan Kaur*, Mia Singh, Hari Singh

Khalifa

Waryam Singh 'Khalifa'

Gurbachan Kaur

Khalifa

A special railway train bearing the Kenya National and the Sikh emblem flags, was arranged for the onwards journey from Kisumu to Makindu.
Waryam Singh 'Khalifa' was one of the founding fathers of the Sikh Temple at Makindu.

Khalifa

Punjabi Farm

www.ingramcontent.com/pod-product-compliance
Lightning Source LLC
Chambersburg PA
CBHW041757040426
42446CB00001B/66